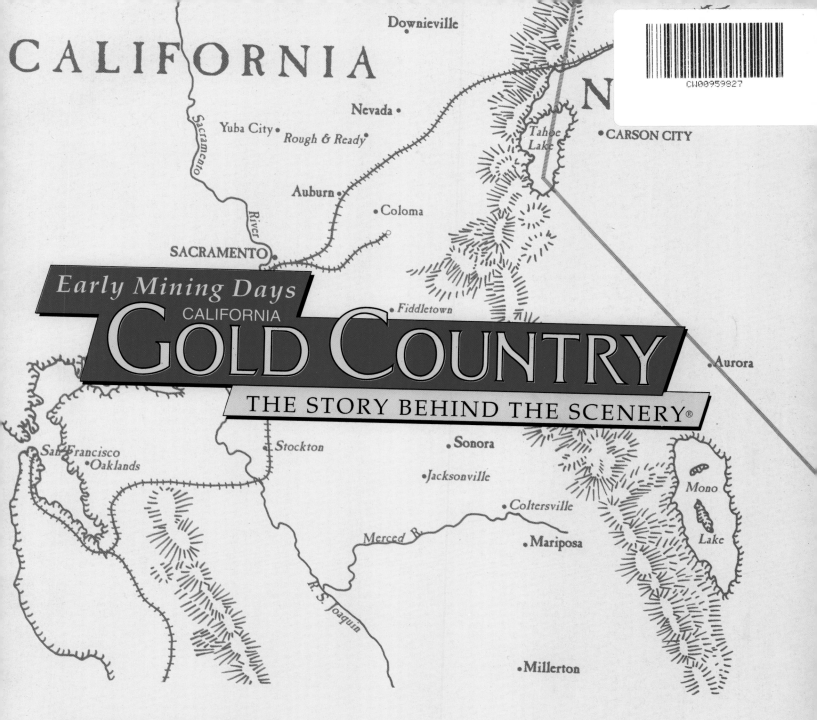

CALIFORNIA

Downieville

Nevada •

Yuba City •

Rough & Ready•

Sacramento River

Auburn •

• Coloma

SACRAMENTO

NEVADA

Tahoe Lake

• CARSON CITY

Early Mining Days
CALIFORNIA
GOLD COUNTRY
THE STORY BEHIND THE SCENERY®

• Fiddletown

• Aurora

San Francisco
• Oaklands

Stockton

• Sonora

•Jacksonville

• Coltersville

Merced R.

Mono

•Mariposa

Lake

R. S. Joaquin

• Millerton

Text by Stanley W. Paher

Stanley W. Paher has written 21 books about mining camps and ghost towns, which have become established reference materials. Here, Jerry Bowen, an enthusiastic researcher of the Mother Lode, collaborated with him in writing about California's gold rush.

Photography by Ed Cooper

An avid photographer, hiker and climber, Ed Cooper, at age 30, left the confining financial canyons of Wall Street to make photography his career — he hasn't looked back since.

Front cover: Illustration from the author's collection.
Inside front cover: Old Stamp Mill at Mariposa Museum. Pages 2/3: Sierra Buttes.

Edited by Mary L. Van Camp. Book design by K.C. DenDooven.

First Printing, 1996
EARLY MINING DAYS - CALIFORNIA GOLD COUNTRY: THE STORY BEHIND THE SCENERY.
© 1996, KC PUBLICATIONS, INC. LC 96-75337. ISBN 0-88714-111-0.

*G*old! *The reason for the great migration*
westward to the foothills of California's
Sierra Nevada in '49. The new gold region produced
its share of adventure, romance, and history
of a people who struggled to realize their share
of the American dream.

The Gold Rush to California

Almost a century and a half have passed since the argonauts, commonly known as the "'49ers," scoured the streambeds and hillsides of California's Mother Lode in search of gold. They had come because of a seemingly insignificant event along a solitary streambed on the American River, the discovery of gold at Coloma early in 1848. This event created a mining excitement and a subsequent emigration which changed the lives of people the world over.

Just who were the '49ers? From the comforts and conveniences of our modern-day lifestyle we can view with a romantic eye the glamour and adventure of pioneer life without experiencing the kick of a mule, bedding infested with bedbugs and fleas, rancid food and unfamiliar meat, or the perils of would-be highwaymen or claim jumpers. What made these hardy folks risk so much to emigrate across the country to a virtually unknown land, Alta California? Understanding comes from looking back at the time before the '49ers invaded it.

Rumors of gold in New Spain, which includes all of present-day California, existed as far back as 1577, when Captain Francis Drake, the privateer, beached his frigate in a California bay to make repairs. Whether knowledge of gold in the strange land was gained from personal exploration or from the native Indians still remains unknown. At any rate, the ship's chaplain, Francis Fletcher, upon his return to the old world, spread the rumor of the precious metal all over London. With the eventual discovery of San Francisco Bay in 1769, interest in California began to grow and rumors of gold and riches beyond belief persisted without any factual evidence.

In 1774, the Franciscan fathers of the Catholic Church established a chain of mission outposts in the southwest. They soon spread northward, culminating in the Mission San Francisco de Solano at Sonoma in 1823. These men did a remarkable job in creating small but rich agricultural communities. But, a church-ruled economy was obsolete, even in 1821 when Mexico revolted against mother Spain.

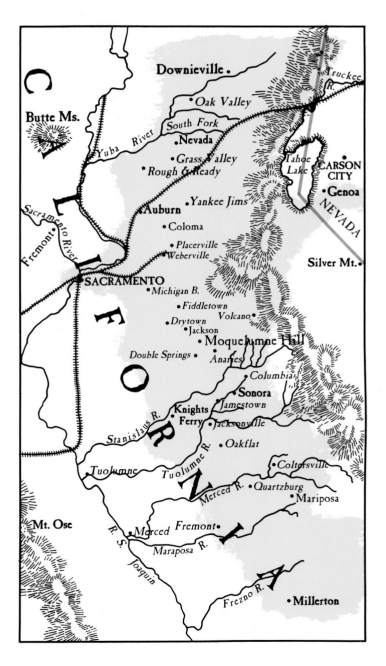

◁ *Wherever the great Mother Lode belt of gold-bearing veins extended, mining camps came into existence, as partially shown in this map of 1871. Today's modern California State Highway 49, the Gold Rush Highway, threads its way through this nine-county area, which at one time or another contained more than 2,500 mining camps and towns. Most have disappeared without even the faintest of traces, with only descriptive names remaining on maps—places such as Bedbug, Whiskey Slide, Fleatown, and Bloody Gulch to name a few. But what has been left behind is a legacy rich with legend and history.*

"The love of money is the root of all evil—with the love of other things added. Forty years ago the gold mines of California was all the talk, and the 'gold fever' was as contagious as the itch, and if you took it, brimstone and grease wouldn't cure you. The only remedy was for you to go to the mines and try your luck."

—Pioneer Memoir of John Berry Hill.

With the passing of Spanish rule, California could easily have become the victim of the predatory design of any large 19th century nation. Indeed, the Russians had a foothold at Fort Ross to the north of San Francisco and Britain had a valid claim to California, since Drake had actually taken possession many years before at Point Reyes. French and English trappers were joined by the Americans and established trade routes which were destined to become emigrant trails and pathways to California.

As time passed, additional rumors of gold surfaced. As early as 1814, trappers told of mining operations by the Spanish settlers in southern California at the Potholes and in the Cargo Muchacho Mountains near the lower reaches of the Colorado River. H.H. Bancroft recorded an early gold discovery in the San Fernando Valley in the following account: "A version of the discovery is that in the early part of 1840, Don Andreas Castillero, a Mexican mineralogist, picking up a pebble [and] remarked that wherever these stones were found gold must exist." Francisco Lopez overheard the observation and remembered it when some months later, while plucking wild onions, he found a similar pebble in the earth that proved to be a grain of gold. Even with the shipping of about 20 ounces of gold from this area to the U.S. Mint at Philadelphia in 1841, the discovery of gold passed with little notice.

EMIGRANTS ARRIVE

The first emigrant train to actually enter California was the Bartleson-Bidwell Party in 1841. Several other wagons of adventurers followed, and the long-entrenched Mexicans soon became alarmed at the influx of Americans. Eventually re-lations were strained to the breaking point, culminating in the Bear Flag Revolt which placed California under defacto American control in 1846.

John A. Sutter, a Swiss emigrant, arrived in California in 1839 with a dream of building his own colony, New Helvetia. He filed for Mexican citizenship and built Sutter's Fort (at present-day Sacramento) near the confluence of the American and Sacramento rivers. Sutter continued to add to his holdings and became one of California's more influential figures. But a fateful decision to hire a carpenter, John Marshall, to build a sawmill 50 miles to the east on the South Fork of the American River in 1847, would eventually spell the end to his dreams.

Marshall hired a group of Mormon settlers to build a sawmill on a site later to be named Coloma. Everything went slowly until January 24, 1848, when Marshall picked up a piece of metal he believed to be gold in the tailrace of the mill. A very excited Marshall rushed to Sutter's Fort to inform his employer of his discovery. They tested the metal and were convinced it was indeed gold.

Fearing news of the discovery would ruin him, "Captain" John Sutter pledged James Marshall and the other men to secrecy. Nevertheless, the word slowly leaked out. On March 15, 1848, the *Californian* newspaper at Monterey reported "Gold Mine Found. In the newly made race-way of the sawmill recently erected by Captain Sutter, on the American fork, gold has been found in considerable quantities. One person brought in thirty dollars worth . . . gathered there in a short time." Sam Brannan declared the discovery a sham in his San Francisco newspaper, *The California Star*, but nevertheless gold specimens began to show up in San Francisco, delighting curious people who wanted

to see the ore for themselves and confirm the rumors. The excitement began to grow, and in August, 1848, the news of gold in California reached the New York press.

THE RUSH WAS ON!

By December, the port cities along the nation's eastern seaboard were swarming with eager would-be argonauts who dropped almost everything to journey to California. The rush was on! As well stated by one emigrant, John Berry Hill, " . . . the gold mines of California was all the talk, and the gold fever was as contagious as the itch. . . . The only remedy was for you to go to the mines and try your luck."

The first arrivals knew very little about gold mining, but in the beginning the virgin territory yielded its treasure easily. Mining tools usually consisted of a knife, a shovel, and a bowl or pan which had sloping edges. Nuggets were pried from the crevices of rocks, and dirt shoveled from the creeks and rivers was swirled in the pans to recover the wealth. Crime was virtually non-existent and respect for one another ran high. It was not unusual for a merchant to trust a stranger to pay for goods "sometime," as evident in the following account by Mahlon Fairchild:

The greater part of the forenoon succeeding our arrival at Sacramento was devoted to procuring an outfit for the mines. We needed provisions, picks, shovels, rocker and pan everything. And we had no money by this time, or so little that it did not count toward paying for what we required. Besides the teamster's charge was thirty-five cents a pound freight to our ob-

jective point. There were numerous merchants with goods in tents and in the open scattered promiscuously. We explained the financial condition to the teamster, who said it was all right, that he would trust us until he made another trip. Then we approached a merchant, unrobed our impecuniosity, and he smiled telling us to order whatever he had that we wanted and to pay for it when we could. And we took a goodly supply, and the merchant took no note. I mention these circumstances to show you the temper of the times. The teamster was paid upon his next trip, and the merchant the first time we saw him which was in the month of October, 1851. When we called to pay him he had forgotten the amount of his due, did not remember our name, and could with difficulty recall the transaction. The amount we paid was several hundred dollars.

After 1850, the year California became a state, gold was becoming increasingly more difficult to find. More people crowded into the already overpopulated mining country and a less desirable element had become firmly entrenched. Saloons, gambling establishments, and ladies of the line were the main source of entertainment for the lonely miners.

An interesting observation of the typical '49er was made in 1857 by J.D. Borthwick in his book "Three Years in California":

I became aware that a most ragamuffinish individual was looking over my shoulder. He was certainly, without exception, the most tattered and torn man I ever saw in my life; even his hair and beard gave the idea of rags, which was fully realized by his costume. He was a complete caricature of an old miner, and quite a picture by himself, seen from any point of view.

Contrary to modern novels and westerns, the typical miner dressed plainly wearing clothes readily available. Today's romanticized notions about panning for gold are contradicted by harsh realities of a bleak environment where men toiled long hours in quest of riches.

The rim of his old brown hat seemed ready to drop down on his shoulders at a moment's notice, and the sides, having dissolved all connection with the crown, presented at the top a jagged circumference, festooned here and there with locks of light brown hair, while to keep the whole fabric from falling to pieces of its own weight, it was bound with a piece of string in lieu of a hat band. His hair hung all over his shoulders in large straight flat locks, just as if a handkerchief had been nailed to the top of his head and then torn to shreds, and a long beard of the same pattern fringed from a face as brown as a mahogany table. His shirt had once been red flannel-of course it was flannel yet, what remained of it-but it was in a most dilapidated condition. Halfway down to his elbows hung some shreds, which led to the belief that at one time he had possessed a pair of sleeves . . . There was enough of his shirt left almost to meet a pair of not-trousers . . . He must have had trousers at one time, but I suppose he had worn them out; and I could not help thinking what extraordinary things they must have been on the morning when he came to the conclusion that they were not good enough to wear . . . His boots . . . were more holes than leather.

He was a man between thirty and forty, and, notwithstanding his rags, there was nothing in his appearance at all dirty or repulsive; on the contrary, he had a very handsome, prepossessing face, with an air about him which at once gave the idea that he had been used to polite society.

With the maturation of mining for gold on the Mother Lode, the miners developed new methods of prospecting and mineral extraction. Throughout central California new settlements and towns sprang into being as the miners needed supplies and sources for food. Many of the emigrants engaged in the business of transferring goods, or operating trading posts; others became ranchers and farmers. Paths that started as mere trails turned into roads and highways, and ultimately railroads were also laid to serve the central mining region. The wild rush of '49 began to wane in the mid-1850s, as the gold played out and methods to extract it actually became counter-productive. After 1859, gold and silver discoveries in Nevada drew away the most experienced miners and business people. Despite the recession, California was coming of age.

So who were these individuals called '49ers? After all is said and done, they were nothing more than ordinary men, women and children with dreams and desires much the same as today. Challenging conditions drove them to levels of endurance and achievement they never dreamed possible. They were equal to the challenges and contributed to the future and comforts that modern society takes so much for granted today.

The Central Mines

In this area of the Mother Lode, known as the Central Mines, are the great mining counties with the romantic names of Placer and El Dorado, the latter named for the fabled land of immense wealth associated with the long-established mythical South American Indian chieftain known as the "guilded man." Placer County took its name from the ubiquitous mining technique that involved recovering gold from the gravel in the area's numerous rivers and streams running through deep forested canyons.

As the gold-bearing rock washed away from mountainsides, it tumbled down the numerous streambeds into areas where eager miners recovered the precious metal through the use of rockers, sluices, and the simple but effective gold pan. These adventurers lived in not only the larger towns of Auburn, Georgetown, and Placerville, but also in mining camps with such colorful designations as Poverty Bar, Tryagain Tunnel, Pole Cat Slide, Mad Canyon Diggings, and Temperance Flat.

The central mines, the heart of the Mother Lode, were the focal point of the mid-19th century California gold rush. With the simple words uttered by James Marshall on January 24, 1848, "Boys, by

Sketches or photographs of James Marshall in his youth are unknown. Throughout his life, constant harassment turned Marsha into an embittered man as happiness and fulfillment eluded him. Marshall's wood-frame residence at Coloma stands protected on the grounds of the Marshall Gold Discovery State Historical Park. The cabin is periodically open to visitors who may view replicas of austere furniture consisting of tables and chairs, and contemporary tools. A simple wood-burning stove was Marshall's only source of heat.

▲ **On a hill high above the gold discovery** site is a statue of James Marshall, erected in 1890. Marshall is pointing to the Sutter's Mill, the very place where gold was discovered on January 24, 1848.

God I believe I have found a gold mine," the rush to California was inevitable. Since that eletrifying moment, the blending of factual history and myth has become synonymous with the great emigration to California in search of instant wealth.

When Marshall first discovered gold, only about 2,000 Americans were scattered throughout California. A year and a half later that figure grew to nearly 15,000. By 1853, an estimated 300,000 people of various nationalities were present on or near the Mother Lode. The Lode was in a constant state of flux, as mining camps, farms, and other communities were settled and resettled. San Francisco itself was at times populous and nearly deserted, and at one time its busy harbor was clogged with more than 500 ships, most of them abandoned by their crews and left to decay.

Coloma was the first mining town to emerge in the central mining region. Coloma Road, the original trail opened by Marshall, funneled the invading horde from Sutter's Fort at Sacramento by way of the town of Folsom to Coloma and the gold fields. The population of Coloma rose sharply as additional placer gold discoveries were made. No one was immune to the excitement, as especially evident in the sermon of a Coloma preacher who ended the morning assembly with, "There will be a divine service in this house next Sabbath—if, in the meantime, I hear of no new diggins."

By the summer of 1848, Coloma had a wood frame hotel, 300 buildings under construction, and a population approaching 2,000. Prices for the

◁ **The gold-laden South Fork of the** American River innocently flowed past where gold was discovered by James Marshall in 1848. Although welcome to pan for gold on this site, modern-day recreational miners only occasionally find "colors" here.

◁ **A**mong the Mother Lode's most populous mining camps was the crude community of Hangtown which later became the stable community of Placerville. Among its numerous fine residences was the Combellack-Blair House built in 1895, still a private residence. Many other gold-rush-era buildings on Main Street remain to delight today's curious visitors.

simplest of supplies soared to exorbitant levels; more fortunes were being made by men engaging in commerce, rather than toiling in the scorching sun and miserable rain in search of the yellow metal. After Coloma, more discoveries led to the establishment of other mining camps and towns and, with each shift in population, wagon routes used by teamsters had to be constantly rerouted. Never satisfied with the amount of gold they were finding at the time, most miners, at the slightest word of a new discovery, would leave behind potential fortunes and head to new and richer "diggins" which were often only a few miles away. Prospectors swarmed the hillsides, and with each strike the rumor mills ground anew.

One of these restless persons was Charles Weber. In the spring of 1848, he discovered gold along Weber Creek south of present-day Placerville. He together with Indian Chief Jose Jesus established a trading post and bartered cheap goods for nuggets found by local Indians. Along with others, Weber engaged in intensive

◁ **F**ires were the constant scourge of the gold country's wooden mining camps. Volunteer fire compar built their own buildings and maintained equipment. The firehouse at Fiddletown has a false front, typical of the western mining era.

△ **From crude, generally homemade wagons that brought the emigrants westward, the** '49ers used these sturdier built wagons on display at Coloma to transport goods, machinery, and other supplies among the settlements.

prospecting in the Central Mother Lode and opened up many significant placer gold fields. From this humble beginning, the mining camp of Weberville grew around many promising gold finds. However, the decline came just as swiftly and Weber left the area to become the founding father of Stockton, in the great valley below. Weberville disappeared completely when newer and bigger discoveries were made to the north by William Daylor on Hangtown Creek.

SUCCESSES AND FAILURES

The new mining camp, originally called "Old Dry Diggings" was renamed "Hangtown" after the residents held a necktie party to dispatch three of the local riffraff by hanging them high from a tree. Early in 1849 they had robbed an old man of $6,000 in gold and, in those days, evidently justice was swift and final.

By 1850, Hangtown settled into a more orderly existence, and in 1854 the citizens, tired of the constant notoriety, renamed the town Placerville. John M. Studebaker arrived in town in the middle of August the previous year and began building wheelbarrows, carts, and some

tools for miners. Five years later, "Wheelbarrow John" had acquired a nest egg of $8,000 and returned home to South Bend, Indiana, to establish with his brother the Studebaker Wagon Company, a firm that manufactured automobiles later in the 19th century. Other notables who resided for brief periods of time in Placerville were the hotel executive Mark Hopkins, Philip Armour of meat-packing fame, and the famous stage driver Hank Monk, who gave renowned New York Publisher Horace Greeley the stage ride of his life.

After three disastrous fires visited the town in 1856, Placerville swiftly declined, especially as the nearby gold fields had begun to yield less. The 1859 silver discovery on the Comstock Lode in "Washoe," soon renamed Nevada, reversed the fortunes of Placerville virtually overnight. The Placerville Road, today's modern Highway 50, became the major supply route to the new silver mining boom camp of Virginia City. As described by J. Ross Browne in 1860 during a visit to the Comstock Lode, it was ". . . in a mess of confusion." Now the citizens of Placerville made new fortunes as innkeepers and purveyors of

dry goods, and thus the town avoided the moribund fate of most of the other Mother Lode mining communities.

Discoveries expanded the central mining region rapidly from 1848 to 1850. A Frenchman, Claude Chana, had been working for John Sutter as a cooper since 1846, but eventually John Marshall showed him how to pan for gold. Bitten by the gold bug, Chana tried his luck on the Yuba River early in 1848, much to the disgust of Sutter. But for Chana it was a wise decision for he made a quick $25,000. Chana eventually discovered gold in what became known as Rich Ravine. With an influx of population, it was renamed successively Rich Dry Diggings, North Fork Dry Diggings, Woods Dry Diggings and, finally in August 1849, Auburn. The new community earned the nickname "three story town" because the townsite spread over three distinct levels of elevation. At the peak of the rush in 1849-50,

◁ **In Auburn's Old Town the distinctive** wood-frame firehouse with belfry, originally built in 1891, stands by itself near a monument honoring the early day gold panner.

⚒ **By 1860, Auburn was a substantial community as shown in this magnificent panorama which was** drawn before the arrival of the Central Pacific Railroad in 1865. Distinctly shown to the right of center is Auburn's commercial district, now in the area of present-day Old Town.

Auburn had a population of about 1,300, and many gold miners using sluices and rockers made $1,200 to $1,500 a day.

North of Placerville and southeast of Auburn is Georgetown, where gold was discovered along Oregon Creek and Hudson Gulch in the summer of 1849. A collection of tents and crude cabins was thrown up along the foot of today's Main Street. In 1849-50 this settlement was called "Growlersburg." Two stories are given for the name. One source insists it was named by its happier citizens for the few grumblers or "growlers" of the new mining community. Another popular story credits the name of the town to the sound made by large nuggets while they swirled with the dirt in a miner's pan. Come what may, the difference is only one of many to show why it is difficult to separate myth from historical fact.

Fire destroyed the original town and abandonment followed in 1852 in favor of the present site on the hill to the east, at which time it took the name Georgetown. There was very little crime, although a Mr. Devine was hung here for killing his wife. He had justified his act because

she would not give him a $900 nugget they owned to pay off a bar bill, so he could resume drinking. The town hung him "with great reluctance," but carried out the sentence anyway because "it was the right thing to do."

Georgetown did not suffer a fiery fate as did so many other gold rush towns, because its founders had wisely decided to lay out a very wide main street. Along it are many buildings dating from the 19th century, including some structures from the earliest days of the gold rush.

Many other mining towns sprang up in the central mining region, each with their own stories and legends—places such as Shingle Springs, Diamond Springs, El Dorado, Dutch Flat, and Colfax still exist and continue to grow. At some future time they may become the suburbs of larger cities, while others such as Michigan Bluff, Foresthill, and Lotus are still far removed from state and federal highways. Thus they will retain their gold-rush atmosphere and charm for the visitor traveling the Gold Rush Highway and its side roads.

⚒

◁ △ **In the fledgling California gold-mining** camps before 1850, civility reigned. Yet, within just a year or two, attitudes changed with the influx of gamblers, ne'er-do-wells, and desperados, bringing about the need for the hangman's noose. In every county law enforcement consisted of the sheriff and a few deputies—their practice was necessarily simple and efficient. A wood-frame courthouse was built at Auburn soon after the creation of Placer County in 1851. Later, in the 1890s, it was replaced by a stately structure of sandstone and brick constructed on a hill at the site of the early public square that also served as the hanging location. This courthouse has been in constant use. At left is an iron jail cell formerly used in the El Dorado County Courthouse at Placerville. It is now on display at the state park in Coloma.

△ **T***he Napa wine country* *does not have a monopoly on winemaking—near Placerville are many vineyards including the gold-rush-era Boeger Winery which distills grapes harvested from the nearby rolling hills.*

S*tout stone walls show the* *location of windows and the door to the two-story Zeisz Brewery, once complete with balconies, built in 1852 to satisfy the thirst of the earliest settlers on the Mother Lode. Less than ten years later, area breweries increased their business by busily supplying local lodging houses which refreshed the eager silver-mad crowd en route to Virginia City, Nevada.*

◁ **Among the prominent** buildings at Georgetown, dating from the mid-19th century, are the dwellings, the armory, the IOOF Hall, and the former American Hotel, first erected in 1863 and rebuilt at century's end. It is still open for guests. Georgetown has held on through the years and today it is among California gold country's more charming towns, despite being surrounded by modern development.

In a depression created ▷ during the mid-19th-century days of hydraulic mining, this pool still shows some evidence of mineralization. This Immense industry carved up hillsides and ravines, leaving behind debris-filled rivers and farmlands. Of the estimated yield of $614 million in gold recovered along the Mother Lode during the first 25 years of its existence, the majority of it came as a result of hydraulic mining.

⚒ **Early eastern journalists who may** have journeyed to the California gold fields wrote and sketched the activity for publication in East Coast newspapers. The most famous of them, Horace Greeley of New York, observed that California's entire economy was quickened by mining. Everywhere he went throughout the Mother Lode he was seldom a mile away from past or present "diggings." Every ravine, gully, and water course had been prospected at some time and opened to bedrock, and the earth or gravel run through a rocker (shown at right) or sluice or panned "in hope of making it yield the shining dust." Known as the discoverer of gold in Placer County's Auburn Ravine early in 1849, French emigrant Claude Chana soon moved on after making his fortune. Nevertheless, his work is memorialized by a monument situated in Auburn's Old Town.

17

The Northern Mines

At the northern end of the Mother Lode are located the great mining centers of Nevada City and Grass Valley, two gold-bearing districts which for decades consistently yielded the precious metal. These are joined by San Juan, Downieville, Rough and Ready, You Bet, Red Dog, Little York, and Eureka, as well as nearly 400 other places in Nevada County alone. A century ago there was a mining camp about every three to four miles along all principal roads and ravines.

Mining in the north began, as always, with the finding of the easily located placer gold. For a considerable time, the gold still encased in the mother rock was ignored due to the lack of knowledge by the first arrivals on the scene. But, as the easily recovered gold was depleted, more experienced miners out of necessity found new ways to extract the great wealth locked deep within the hard rock of the Mother Lode.

Phenomenal growth in the northern area of the Mother Lode first came about because of fabulous surface placer gold discoveries during 1849-50. But by October, 1850, the discovery of rich quartz-bearing veins by George Knight on Gold Hill near Grass Valley, inaugurated quartz mining in California. Immensely rich discoveries led

Central Pacific Railroad stations such as Dutch Flat, Gold Run, and Cisco, were established on the Mother Lode soon after the railroad began running eastward past Auburn. Each of these communities also possessed a couple of hotels, stage office, saloons, and livery stables. Stagecoaches met the trains and whisked passengers and freight to the gold towns, both north and south.

*"$F$are one ounce of gold. Unhesitatingly I
took passage, for I had 'come to California
with my washbowl on my knee,' and
was in a hurry to get to the diggins."*
—Mahlon Fairchild.

Like both ancient Rome and modern San Francisco, which exhibit a most distinguishable
*topographic characteristic, Nevada City is situated on seven diverse hills studded with stately
pines. Quaint 19th-century buildings which have stubbornly resisted modernization line Main Street.
The charming commercial and residential buildings situated throughout the downtown area are
protected by a local historical preservation ordinance.*

to famous mines such as the North Star, Allison Ranch, and Sixteen-to-One. Others, the Empire and North Star mines, have been preserved as museums in the Grass Valley/Nevada City area.

The discoverer of gold, John Marshall of Coloma, should have initiated a life of luxury. In fact many considered Marshall to be a human "good luck charm," and thus hundreds of fortune seekers followed him around the countryside. Though lucky for others, riches would elude the hard-drinking eccentric, John Marshall.

Nevertheless, during one of his prospecting trips in 1848, Marshall unearthed "colors" near Deer Creek. Dissatisfied with what he found he quickly moved on to "better digs." Had Marshall persevered at Deer Creek, he may well have gained the riches he sought.

The diggings at Deer Creek developed rapidly, becoming one of the richest mining districts in the Northern Mines. Marshall left but others stayed. Captain James Pennington and two companions built the first cabin here in late 1849, fol-

lowed by Dr. A.B. Caldwell who opened a store in October on Aristocracy Hill. The area was called Caldwell's Store until a post office was established in 1850 and the platted townsite took the name Nevada City.

A noted confrontation in Nevada City began when a miner started to dig up the road in front of a popular store. As the angered storekeeper yelled for the miner to "Stop digging up the street," he was answered with a sardonic, "There ain't no law against it." The storekeeper pulled a gun and replied, "There is now!" The miner, with new-found wisdom, instantly decided there must be richer digs elsewhere.

Unprecedented growth soon saw Nevada City with 12,000 hustling inhabitants within a year's time. They were of every nationality and occupation and all focused on the gold. Salesmen were everywhere hawking the latest "scientific" devices, many of which promised to find gold. Norwegian telescopes, divining rods, and diving suits were all available to anyone foolish enough to purchase them. Among the more interesting implements were "gold magnets" which were to be worn near the heart; as the prospector approached a source of gold the magnet would, according to the salesman, produce mild electric shocks to the holder.

As time went by, the town developed a more stable population. In 1850, a Madame Penn worked a rocker to obtain money to build a boarding house. This same property was occupied by various inns until the famous Union Hotel was built in 1863, and nearly a century later succumbed to flames.

$2,000 A DAY!

During the 1850s it was not uncommon for a miner to dig $2,000 in gold daily. A new method of mining involved the digging of shallow tunnels to bedrock resulting in many "coyote holes." They were so numerous that Nevada City gained the nickname "Coyoteville."

Unlike the placer beds which dominated most △ *of the Mother Lode, the geology of the Grass Valley mines invited vastly more productive lode mining. Deep shafts were dug to recover gold. An efficient 20-stamp mill was built, together with quarters for miners and the owner's spacious "cottage" fronted by a water fountain.*

About four miles southwest of Nevada City sister community, appropriately named Grass Valley, came into being when a few settlers began harvesting feed-hay. Gold was also discovered here in October 1848, by David Stump and two others but they left that very winter. Later, agriculture took a back seat in the lush valley as miners trespassed farmland in search of more gold. The discovery of quartz gold by George Knight in October 1850, initiated the first large-scale rush into the Grass Valley district.

A person of note who lived in Grass Valley was the Countess of Landsfield, Bavaria, Maria Delores Eliza Rossana Gilbert, better known as Lola Montez. As an entertainer, her spider dance entranced the miners. She was also responsible for promoting the career of Lotta Crabtree, whose beauty and fame as an entertainer surpassed her teacher.

Besides the usual fires and natural disasters, another event that almost crippled the flourishing towns of Nevada City and Grass Valley was the discovery of silver eastward in the direction

◁ *The Catholic cemetery at Grass Valley is the resting place of many immigrant miners, particularly from Ireland and Wales. Ornate ironworks guard this well-preserved headstone from predators.*

of Washoe in 1859. The rush was on to the fabulous Comstock Lode, virtually emptying the towns up and down the Mother Lode. Ironically in the spring of '59, an assay by a Nevada City resident, J. J. Ott, disclosed that the Comstock ore in fact contained extremely rich sulfurets of silver worth up to $3,000 per ton! The ensuing excitement resulted in a mining rush unparalleled since the earliest days of '49, and thousands of merchants, farmers, prospectors, and miners flocked over the Sierra Nevada that very summer.

Downieville, about 45 miles north of Nevada City, is situated in one of the highest, most rugged areas of California. Late in 1849, William "Major" Downie along with Jim Crow (a Kanaka), ten black sailors and another Indian, penetrated this area and built a cluster of log cabins at the junction of two branches of the North Fork Yuba River. The site, which became known as The Forks, soon developed into a busy mining camp where a man could dig a tin cup of gold a day. Accordingly, Downieville naturally acquired the nicknamed "Tin Cup Diggings."

Though there were few women in the mining regions, they were held in high esteem. Nevertheless, Downieville became the first camp to hang a woman for fatally stabbing a miner. In the heat of the moment, a speedy trial was held and "Jaunita" was hung from the local bridge. For years the residents of this mountain community did not dare to mention the hanging, so deep was the shame.

▲ *The Yuba River neatly separates the commercia and residential districts of Downieville. The drive wheel of an ore crusher heightens the mood of this gold rush town on the northernmost part of the Mother Lode. Besides the General Store, Downieville still has the courthouse for Sierra County, a hotel, churches and a museum housed in an old stone building.*

GOLD IN STRANGE PLACES

Other tales from the past had brighter endings. One woman earned the tidy sum of $500 when she discovered gold in the dirt she swept from her earthen kitchen floor. Jim Crow caught a 14-pound salmon and, after cooking it in a kettle, discovered gold in the residue at the bottom of the pot. On another occasion, miners removed $12,000 in gold in 11 days out of a claim only 60 feet square on a site where the courthouse stands today. Last rites were being given to a departed compatriot, when the clergyman noticed several mourners on their hands and knees digging at the loose dirt around the grave. He quickly joined them digging for large nuggets and the body was unceremoniously buried in another spot.

Situated five miles southwest of Nevada City is another town with a fascinating past, Rough and Ready. It received its name when a party of men calling themselves "The Rough and Ready Company" under the leadership of Capt. A.A.

Townsend, settled in the area in September, 1849. Captain Townsend had served under General Zachary (Old Rough and Ready) Taylor, during the Mexican War. They found rich diggings and managed to keep their discovery quiet for a time but the secret leaked out in 1850. On hearing of the latest "big strike," the hordes rushed in and the town developed rapidly.

Early in 1850, while California was being considered for statehood, one of the newcomers, E.F. Brundage, and about 100 men tried to organize the separate state of Rough and Ready. Issuing a pompous proclamation, he called a mass meeting to organize an independent government. The affair was so ridiculous that the more sensible residents of Rough and Ready, after much opposition from about a hundred followers, prevailed and the idea died aborning.

Fire devastated the town of Rough and Ready in 1850, but the town was rebuilt larger and with renewed energy to a community of about 300 buildings. In later years Rough and Ready also benefited from a copper mining boom in nearby Spenceville, a town that survived into the 1930s as an agricultural community only to perish in an unusual manner. During World War II a nearby military base, Camp Beale, needed a model village in which to practice war maneuvers. The deserted Spenceville was modified with German signs and the impact of flying bullets soon destroyed the remains of the old village.

French Corral, located on rugged San Juan Ridge northwest of Nevada City, was one of the first mining camps on San Juan Ridge. A rich placer gold discovery in 1849 led to the founding of a town on the site of a corral built by an earlier

Travelers on State Route 49 may view the ▷ North Fork of the Yuba River for several miles before entering Downieville. This boulder-strewn riverbed brought riches to many of the earliest fortune seekers, and is still the delight of modern recreational gold miners.

A crowded gambling hall provided relief from the tedium of the daily placer mining regimen. Weeks of hard-earned gold were often lost in a single night at a session of playing such ancient card games as chuck-a-luck, three-card-monte, and faro (shown above), as well as common surviving games including twenty-one and poker.

23

Situated ▷
precariously upon a
steep mountain slope,
Sierra City has been
subjected to numerous
snowslides over the
years, as evidenced by
these skewed dwellings.
The Sierra Buttes loom
in the background
above the timberline.

The rugged country surrounding Sierra City contains many open
shafts, evidence of immense lode-mining activity which took place after the
turn of the century. The Kentucky Mine County Historic Park near
▽ Sierra City preserves a trestle that allows ore-laden cars to travel to the mi

◁ **Preceding Pages.**
Early day gold recovery
techniques include a
rocker beside the stream,
a gold pan filled with water
and gold-bearing gravel and,
at left, the Spanish-style
arrastra wherein an animal
walking about a circular path
drove a cross-arm to which
large boulders were chained.
As the ore was crushed by
the weight of the huge
stones, smaller particles
containing gold then could be
recovered. Illustration from
the author's collection.

26

French resident. Little remains today to show that about 1,000 people inhabited the town during the gold rush.

As is true of many of the old towns, French Corral has its own different claim to fame. In 1878, the Milton Mining and Water Company needed better communication between its widespread operations. Their solution was to build the Ridge Telephone Company from Milton to French Corral, with the main office at North San Juan. Spanning 60 miles, it became among the first long-distance telephone lines in the world.

Many small communities have endured in the northern mining region and the gold rush survives to this day. Recent discoveries of major gold deposits at the Sixteen-to-One Mine near the old gold-rush town of Alleghany have renewed interest in gold mining, although not with the same intensity of the 1800s. New technology has revived the old mine and others once thought to be worked out.

In a letter from C.R. Scholl to his father in Missouri, Oct. 15, 1849, he speculated: "The mines are certainly inexhaustible; and my impression is from what I have seen, that they will be worked until the cycle of ages shall cease to roll." He couldn't have been more correct. Indeed every summer, even a century and a half later, with the spring runoff the canyons are still yielding gold for modern-day professional and recreational prospectors.

Novice gold panners may △ *obtain lessons and tips on the finer techniques of gold panning during visits to celebrations and outings of various gold prospecting organizations. Quick lessons are also available throughout the summer at Columbia State Historical Park.*

◁ *Modern-day gold prospectors also use Hookah air-breathing equipment and dredges to work gold-bearing gravels at the bottom of the North Fork of the Yuba River.*

The old North Star Mine Powerhouse on Wolf
Creek, located at the southern end of Grass Valley, is now the North Star Pelton Wheel Mining Museum. After the spring run-off, the 10-ton wheel with a diameter of 30 feet is a visitors' delight along the creek. The museum also houses a splendid collection of mining illustrations, artifacts, and various ore samples.

Preserving the largest mining operation in ▷
the Grass Valley District, the Empire Mine State Park encompasses a mine that had more or less operated continuously from 1851 until 1957. The Empire has been worked to inclined depths of more than 11,000 feet, producing about $125 million. Invented in 1878, the highly efficient Pelton wheel, recognizable by the many small buckets bolted to its rim, provided power by forcing jets of high-pressure water at the buckets, which in turn operated generators and mining machinery.

△ **The Nevada County Narrow Gauge Railroad served the western part** of Nevada County from 1876 to 1942. It ran between the preeminently mining towns of Nevada City and Grass Valley, and continued another 16 miles southeast to Colfax, a major railroad shipping point on the transcontinental Southern Pacific. Incoming trains brought supplies, equipment, and mining machinery, while outbound trains carried ore and bullion, as well as passengers. The end of the Narrow Gauge came during WWII with the slowdown of gold-mining operations and increased competition from highway carriers. Steam engines and rail cars, tangible reminders of this little-known railroad, are on display in Nevada City.

*S*ince California's ▷ gold deposits were contained in gravel beds in ancient river channels as deep as 500 to 600 feet, and up to half a mile wide, the most expeditious way to recover gold was by blasting away the hills with high-pressure hydraulic giants. This "giant" is on display at Malakoff Diggings State Historic Park.

A former hotel ▷ at Johnsville, built in 1908, is now a private residence at Plumas-Eureka Park. Several other wooden buildings remain at the site of Johnsville, a "Johnny-come-lately" mining camp which dates back only to the 1870s.

◁ **During 1866 to 1884, the** immense amount of hydraulic mining had scarred San Juan Ridge so deeply that even today time has been unable to erase the effect of the early activity. Nevertheless the formations have a beauty of their own and are now encased within Malakoff Diggings State Historic Park. Similar, multicolored cliffs created by man exist at Red Dog, You Bet, Mokelumne Hill and other places in between. Headquarters for Malakoff Diggings is Bloomfield, approximately 6 miles northeast of Nevada City. North Bloomfield itself, a town that had 1,200 people in 1880, has been reduced to a pleasant hamlet with not even one store.

Dating from the 1870s, ▷ the Mohawk Stamp Mill in Plumas-Eureka State Park is a picturesque, off the beaten path ruin in a remarkably good state of preservation. The mill built of wood has withstood the ravages of severe winters and vandals.

The Southern Mines

The Southern Mines is the land of Bret Harte, Mark Twain, Fremont, Murrietta, and an international potpourri of Mexican, Chinese, Australian, and European gold miners. Many names of old towns and mining camps reflect the international mix of the people who built them. Sonora, Chinese Camp, Hornitos, Murphy's, Chile Gulch, and Campo Seco are reminders of a past rich in history and lore. In this area is one of the gold country's best preserved mining towns, Columbia, which soon became known as the "Gem of the Southern Mines."

As a result of the great gold discovery at Coloma, rich placer gold finds were made in the area today known as the southern mines. In fact, in the summer of 1848 more than 4,000 prospectors were combing the foothills around present-day Columbia and Jackson. When George Angel built a trading post on Calavaritas Creek, Angels Camp was born. After four Frenchmen made monumental finds at Mokelumne

> "...*S*uch is the character of the American people, that they will never stop their researches until every foot of earth in this vast El Dorado has been prospected to the bedrock and two hundred years from this time will find the Yankees digging for gold on the western slope of the Sierra Nevada."
>
> —*Franklin Street, 1850*

FROM THE AUTHOR'S COLLECTION

In the evening, over an open campfire and beneath tall trees, Mother Lode miners discuss their day's finds while cooking a simple meal, probably consisting of beans, bacon, and available game.

Although the Kennedy Mine dates from ~~~he~~ mid-1850s, the tailing wheels were not installed ~~~ntil~~ 1914 to ease the task of removing tailings ~~~rom~~ the Kennedy Mill. Each wheel contains 16 spokes, ~~~"~~x10" in size, and are made of Oregon pine. ~~~Of~~ the four original wheels, only two stand erect ~~~nd~~ are easily found north of Jackson.

Hill, another mining camp came to life. Mexicans, more experienced than the new arrivals, found gold at Shaw's Flat and Sonora, then known as Sonorian Camp.

Chile Gulch, two miles south of Mokelumne Hill, rose from the efforts of South American prospectors who first mined there. Until the fall of 1849, when cold weather set in, trading posts and mining camps were established throughout the southern end of the Mother Lode.

The twisting route of modern Highway 49 harbors interesting reminders of the gold rush. A stop at Murphy's, near Angels Camp, is a pilgrimage into the past. The main street is lined with numerous wooden and stone buildings that date back to gold-rush days. The Sperry-Perry Hotel, built in 1855 by James Sperry (later of Sperry flour fame) and John Perry still exists. Later renamed Murphy's, this hotel had distinguished visitors such as President U.S. Grant, Horatio Alger, Mark Twain, Henry Ward Beecher, Thomas Lipton, J. Pierpont Morgan, and even Thomas Bolton, who was better known as Black Bart — all of these names and more grace the aging pages of Murphy's ledger.

"WARS" AND BANDITS

One of the claims to notoriety of the southern mines were the "wars" that occurred here. The Chinese, normally hard working people who kept to themselves, split into two warring Tong factions at a mining camp appropriately named Chinese Camp. Opponents made preparations for months for a Tong war which would be held at a specified date. Weapons were meticulously assembled for the engagement. The word spread among neighboring camps, and curious miners gathered to witness the expected bloodbath. On a

33

▲ **In a restful, tree-studded setting, primitive Indian** *dwellings at Indian Grinding Rock Park have been reconstructed near the site of a large limestone grinding rock. Miwok Indian women would use a 14,000-square-foot rock as a community gristmill to grind nuts and berries into meal. More than 1,000 mortar holes remain in that ancient grinding rock. Hundreds of petroglyphs can also be seen in the area.*

flat plain outside of Chinese Camp, about 2,000 fervent Asian warriors clashed in a great maelstrom of noise, clanging and shouting. When the battle was over there were only eight casualties and no one ever did figure out who won.

In another incident, American miners objected to a Chilean aristocrat who sewed up large areas of the Mokelumne River by using his peons as mining claimants. The miners passed a set of laws prohibiting the practice, and forthwith sent an emissary to order the Chileans to leave the district. A few nights later, the Chileans, with blanket warrant in hand signed by a drunken Stockton judge, rounded up the American miners in the area, killing two who resisted, and started marching them westward in the direction of Stockton. But one night during the march, the miners slipped their bonds and turned the tables on their captors. After gaining the upper hand, the now victorious miners nevertheless continued on to Stockton to locate the judge. After sobering up and realizing what he had done, the judge dis-

creetly disappeared. Justice prevailed and the two Chileans who had killed the Americans were expeditiously found guilty and hung. Several of the others were flogged, and two of them were punished by cutting their ears off.

Near Mokelumne Hill in 1850, seven Frenchmen found good "diggins" and spread the word to their countrymen. Scores of Frenchmen took over the immediate area and raised the tricolor French flag on the knoll above the mining camp of Mok (Mokelumne) Hill. Naturally, the Americans upon hearing of the fabulous finds by the "Frenchies" made attempts to infiltrate the territory. Rebuffed, the Americans became bel-

The locustlike Trees of Heaven surround the ▷ long-standing post office at Chinese Camp, a community in the center of a large district that contained as many as 5,000 Chinese at the height of the gold rush. This post office, built in 1854, functioned until 1984. Nearby contemporary ruins include the Wells Fargo building, another store, and a cemetery.

ligerent, and so the French dispatched couriers far and wide for reinforcements. A skirmish appeared imminent when the Americans hauled a useless ancient Spanish cannon to the hill. The bluff worked and the French lowered their flag in surrender, ending the war.

Bandits flourished in many places as the gold rush entered its second year, 1850. One of them, the well-known Joaquin Murietta had traveled all the way from Sonora, Mexico, and settled in the mining camp of Murphy's. After being accused of cheating at cards, he was tied to a tree and whipped; his wife was assaulted, and his brother was killed by the Americans. Thereafter, Joaquin Murietta retaliated by devoting himself to murder and highway robbery with many crimes attributed to him over a large area of California. More likely, there were perhaps as many as five Mexican bandits who committed the crimes blamed on Murietta.

In hunting down the bandits in 1853, Captain Harry Love was paid a reward for bringing in the supposed head of Joaquin Murietta, as well as the hand of "Three Fingered Jack," another notorious desperado. The pickled

human evidence was displayed throughout the state, disappearing during the great San Francisco earthquake and fire of 1906. Separating myth from fact is almost impossible, but such stories are the ingredients of which Mother Lode legend and lore are made.

Among the burgeoning mining districts was Columbia, which by 1850 became California's second largest town. The camp formed when a group of Mexicans settled here after being forced off their claims in Sonora but, unfortunately for them, after making another strike, they were

From its beginnings ▷ as a small Mexican placer mining camp in the 1850s, Campo Seco was at its height in the 1860s, when the Penn Copper Mine was active. This building of adobe and stone attests to the earlier activity.

On Jackass Hill, ▷
near Tuttletown, is the
reconstructed Gillis
brothers' cabin, called
the Mark Twain
cabin because the
humorist resided at this
place briefly in
1864, as told in his
famous book.
Twain describes the
California gold
seekers as a "driving,
vigorous, restless
population of nearly
two hundred
thousand people."

again sent on their way. After Dr. Thadeus Hildreth and a few other prospectors discovered gold on Kennebec Hill later in 1850, within a month the area was swarming with almost 5,000 men. The enormously rich diggings, soon to become known as "The Gem of the Southern Mines," averaged more than $100,000 a week and soon Columbia boasted a population in excess of 25,000. Three years later two major fires virtually wiped out the town, but it always returned from the ashes. Soon the town was rebuilt with mostly brick buildings, and now it is one of the Sierra's best preserved mining towns.

Mark Twain

In the spring of 1861, Samuel Clemens arrived in the West and for about a year tried his hand at mining and milling in Nevada territory. Failing to strike it rich, he became city editor of Virginia City's *Territorial Enterprise*. It was here that he first used the name Mark Twain as his nom de plume. He moved to San Francisco in 1864 where he met Bret Harte, a man who published many of Twain's stories in the popular *Overland Monthly*. Early in 1865, Twain moved in with the Gillis brothers on Jackass Hill about 17 miles southeast of Angels Camp near Tuttletown, trying his hand at pocket mining. One day Twain listened to Ben Coon, an old Mississippi River pilot, as he told a story of a jumping frog contest won by loading one of the competing amphibians with buck shot. Based on that tale he later wrote "The Celebrated Jumping Frog of Calaveras County," a short story that became a literary success.

Years later in 1928, the Angels Booster Club successfully celebrated the completion of the first paved road into Angels Camp by holding a "Jumping Frog Jubilee" cashing in on the fame generated by the story. The town was jammed with visitors, and since then the "Calaveras County Fair and Frog Jump" has been the biggest annual event of the southern gold region.

Another notable western figure who tried to gain riches by mining in the southern region was John C. Fremont. After years of western exploration, he settled in the California foothills after a friend had purchased a huge expanse of land called the Mariposas Rancho for him. At first, Fremont was unhappy with the location, but he soon realized that there was a potential for gold on the property after hearing about the strike in Coloma. Gold mining paid well for Fremont and his wife, Jesse, but others hearing of the "rich diggins" in the south, soon trespassed on the Fremont property and began mining for gold. Unable to control the invading horde, he finally gave up trying to stop them, and thereafter pursued other interests, including politics. Fremont was the first vice-presidential nominee of the newly formed Republican party in 1856. In the long run he lost everything and died a broken man in 1890.

△ **At Utica Park in Angels Camp, a larger-**
*than-life statue of Mark Twain memorializes
the place where Twain overheard in a bar the
story about a jumping frog contest.*

△ **Still another western personage associated with**
*California gold country is Col. John C. Fremont who
made his headquarters at Rancho Las Mariposas in Bear
Valley. Other nearby ruins of interest include stores,
a saloon, a boarding house, and a Chinese settlement
reduced to stone remains.*

MOTHER LODE HISTORY SURVIVES

The southern mining region of the Mother
Lode is the gateway to the now popular Yosemite
National Park. The history of the Mother Lode
has survived the vicissitudes of economic and
population shifts and the passing of many
decades, and its historic treasures have survived
the ravages of time. It can be truly said that the
Mother Lode region has something to please the
tastes of almost everyone. This entire region is
bountifully endowed with the natural beauty of
California and a pleasant climate that attracts visitors from the world over. The naked rocks left
exposed to the discerning eye serve to remind of
the wild rush to riches by the miners. The romantic tales, ghostly remains of towns, and decaying
mine and mill buildings will continue to prod the
visitor to "dig a little deeper" into the history
along the fabulous Gold Rush Highway.

SUGGESTED READING

CALIFORNIA DIVISION OF MINES. *Geologic Guidebook along
Highway 49—Sierran Gold Belt.* San Francisco, 1949.
HOLLIDAY, J.S. *The World Rushed In.* New York: Simon and
Schuster, 1981.
NADEAU, REMI. *Ghost Towns and Mining Camps of California.*
Los Angeles: The Ward Ritchie Press, 1965.
STILLMAN, LOUIS J. *Mother Lode.* San Francisco: Harr Wagner
Publishing Co., 1939.

*◁ **In many places the** oak-covered Sierra Nevada foothills are almost as the gold-mad '49ers viewed them a century and a half ago. Outside of the mining camp areas, small ranches and farms flourished. Even today, many individuals who perceive that Jackson, Placerville, and Auburn are growing too fast, now build country homes in such pastoral settings. The day will eventually come when this scene will be a thing of the past.*

*****Built in 1851, the** ▷ Hotel Leger at Mokelumne Hill originally served as the courthouse of Calaveras County from 1852 to 1866. Afterwards, George Leger included it as part of his adjacent hotel. It still serves the dining and lodging public.*

In Volcano, this ▷
imposing building
has been variously
identified as a theater,
sash and door
factory, a double saloon,
clothing store, and
a Wells Fargo office—a
fusion of fact and
myth. Without a doubt,
such an imposing
building was
used for commercial
purposes, probably
a store selling
general merchandise.

◁ **The meeting hall at Fiddletown**
sports a bowed instrument to
publicize its location. Fiddletown is
best known for the rammed earth
Chinese store, one of two remaining
of this type in California, and the
Schallhorne Blacksmith & Wagon Shop.

Although Amador ▷
City began as a mining
camp, its claim of
prominence came about
because a preacher
found quartz-gold
on what became known
as the "Minister's
Claim." Stone and wooden
gold-rush-era
buildings stand amid
modern structures
containing numerous
stores and cafes.

△ **C**opper ore dumps abound at Copperopolis, one of the very few Mother Lode camps not known for producing gold. This district reached its height of production very soon after the Civil War when its nearly 2,000 people supported three schools, four hotels, and numerous businesses.

△ **S**t. Anne's Catholic Church, dating from the mid-1850s, is now part of Columbia State Historic Park.

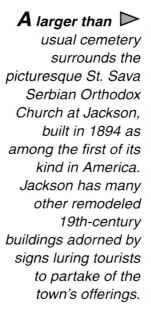

A larger than ▷ usual cemetery surrounds the picturesque St. Sava Serbian Orthodox Church at Jackson, built in 1894 as among the first of its kind in America. Jackson has many other remodeled 19th-century buildings adorned by signs luring tourists to partake of the town's offerings.

◁ *A town falling into disrepair during the mid-20th century, Columbia has rebounded as a restored gold rush town where visitors can ride through its streets of yesteryear on an authentic Wells Fargo stagecoach. The brick two-story building at left is the original Wells Fargo and Co. express office.*

The Lightner Mine at Angels Camp joined the Sultan, Utica, and Stickle mines in early production of quartz bearing gold. The Lightner's hoisting equipment is now on display in a city park whose name, according to ▽ Louis Stillman, "owes its name to neither blasphemy or sentimentality."

△ **Stealing a page from a midwestern road engineer's notebook, various Californians erected covered** bridges at strategic locations. As early as 1863, a covered bridge was built across the Stanislaus River, but was washed away in a later flood. This rebuilt bridge is located near Highway 120/108, south of Copperopolis.

◁ **Dominating this** scene of Sonora is the Tuolumne Courthouse behind it is the steeple of St. Patrick's Catholic Chur Charming Sonora is a popular destination point f city dwellers because of a fine museum, numero century-old business structures, the IOOF build and other restored buildings, and at least a dozen victorian residences including the Street-Morgan building. Four gold rush cemeteries surround the town.

In recent years, bed and breakfast establishments have opened up and down the Mother Lode. At Murphy's, the two-story Dunbar House operates in a building said to have been built in 1880. Fortunately situated away from Highway 49, the town has retained much of its gold-rush-era authenticity. Buildings such as this one are a delight to both the historian and the artist.

Near the southern end of California gold country is Jamestown, whose downtown park sports a gazebo. Behind it is the 1852 Methodist Church, rebuilt early in the 20th century. Jamestown is the headquarters of the Sierra Railroad, which began operating in 1897. Visitors can still enjoy a train ride through interesting mining country.

△ **Hotel Jeffery, on the plaza at Coulterville, is built** upon the site of two preceding structures which succumbed to flames. Other gold-rush-era buildings remain.

◁ **In continuous use since 1854 (although records** show court activity as early as 1850), the Mariposa County Courthouse, in Mariposa, is California's oldest. Yosemite-bound tourists leaving Merced often pass by this historic building as they traverse Highway 140.

Founded as a town ▷ by Mexican miners in 1850, Hornitos still boasts of many structures of historic interest. The red brick Ghirardelli Store was run by the family who later established a chocolate company in San Francisco. Other points of interest at Hornitos are the Wells Fargo office, the Masonic Lodge, a later-built Catholic church, and the town jail.

***S**ituated in the lower* ▷
sections of the Sierra foothills and alongside the Tuolumne River is the community of La Grange, settled by miners in 1852 as a trading center initially known as French Bar. La Grange is said to have had a population estimated at 4,000 before 1860. Among its stone and adobe ruins is this trading post still in fine condition.

***A**lthough freighting was a*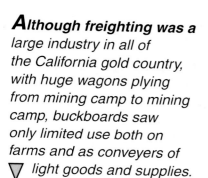
large industry in all of the California gold country, with huge wagons plying from mining camp to mining camp, buckboards saw only limited use both on farms and as conveyers of ▽ *light goods and supplies.*

Yes, there is still GOLD!
on the Mother Lode . . .

▲ **W**ithout a Sutter's Fort, the '49ers *would have encountered initially immense difficulty in procuring supplies while traveling to the gold fields.*

Whereas in the early days the cry was "Gold! Gold in Californy!" producing the greatest migration in the world's history and changing the course of national development forever, the riches of California's gold country now consist of tourism, commercial and recreational gold mining, and the many service industries that support the area.

Tourists will find the mild climate comfortable both in winter and summer and, besides the varied scenery, historic ruins, museums, and state parks, all who venture to California's gold country will find an array of quaint stores and shops for casual browsing and even the serious purchasing of antiques and jewelry. Restaurants of varying quality are found all along Highway 49 and its tributaries. Many fine dinner houses rival those found in well-known metropolitan areas.

To take a true pilgrimage into the past, arrange for overnight stays at any number of old hotels and bed and breakfast establishments. In this way the visitor can acquire a feeling for the gold rush era, and its conviviality of communing in places where the famous of yesteryear ate and slept.

The 120-mile-long Highway 49 crisscrosses many ravines, creeks, and rivers. Hell's Hollow, at the southern end of the gold country, is bisected by the Merced River, the southernmost river on the Mother Lode.

In the very heart of the California gold country, between Angels Camp and Carson Hill is a modern open-pit gold mining operation. Unlike pioneer placer mining operations which often destroyed hillsides with abandon, this modern mining operation must restore disturbed hillsides to nearly parklike status.

Books on national park areas in "The Story Behind the Scenery" series are: Acadia, Alcatraz Island, Arches, Big Bend, Biscayne, Blue Ridge Parkway, Bryce Canyon, Canyon de Chelly, Canyonlands, Cape Cod, Capitol Reef, Channel Islands, Civil War Parks, Colonial, Crater Lake, Death Valley, Denali, Devils Tower, Dinosaur, Everglades, Fort Clatsop, Gettysburg, Glacier, Glen Canyon-Lake Powell, Grand Canyon, Grand Canyon-North Rim, Grand Teton, Great Basin, Great Smoky Mountains, Haleakala, Hawaii Volcanoes, Independence, Lake Mead-Hoover Dam, Lassen Volcanic, Lincoln Parks, Mammoth Cave, Mesa Verde, Mount Rainier, Mount Rushmore, National Park Service, National Seashores, North Cascades, Olympic, Petrified Forest, Redwood, Rocky Mountain, Scotty's Castle, Sequoia & Kings Canyon, Shenandoah, Statue of Liberty, Theodore Roosevelt, Virgin Islands, Yellowstone, Yosemite, Zion.

Additional books in "The Story Behind the Scenery" series are: Annapolis, Big Sur, California Gold Country, California Trail, Colorado Plateau, Columbia River Gorge, Fire: A Force of Nature, Grand Circle Adventure, John Wesley Powell, Kauai, Lake Tahoe, Las Vegas, Lewis & Clark, Monument Valley, Mormon Temple Square, Mormon Trail, Mount St. Helens, Nevada's Red Rock Canyon, Nevada's Valley of Fire, Oregon Trail, Oregon Trail Center, Santa Catalina, Santa Fe Trail, Sharks, Sonoran Desert, U.S. Virgin Islands, Water: A Gift of Nature, Whales.

A companion series of national park areas is the NEW "in pictures...The Continuing Story." This series has **Translation Packages**, providing each title with a complete text both in English and, individually, a second language, German, French, or Japanese. Selected titles in both this series and our other books are available in up to five additional languages.
Call (800-626-9673), fax (702-433-3420), or write to the address below.

Published by KC Publications, 3245 E. Patrick Ln., Suite A, Las Vegas, NV 89120.

Inside back cover: Silhouetted against the setting sun is the Kennedy tailing wheel at Jackson.

Back cover: This hydraulic "Hendy Giant" monitor is preserved in Malakoff Diggings State Historic Park.

Created, Designed and Published in the U.S.A.
Printed by Dong-A Publishing and Printing, Seoul, Korea
Color Separations by Kedia/Kwangyangsa Co., Ltd.